baby animals
Dot-to-Dot

Connect the Dots & Color

D1263806

Evan & Lael Kimble

Sterling Publishing Co., Inc.
New York

This book is dedicated to baby animals, human, domesticated, and wild, and to the hope that there will always be a loving habitat for them.

The following languages are mentioned in this book. People speak differently in different places and so have their own words for things, including animals.

African: one of the languages of Africa

Algonquin: one of the Native American languages

Australian aboriginal language: the language spoken by the people who first lived in Australia.

Cherokee: one of the Native American languages

Cheyenne: one of the Native American languages

Chinese: one of the languages of the Far East

Choctaw: one of the Native American languages

Dakota: one of the Native American languages

Hindi: one of the languages of India

Indonesian: one of the languages of Indonesia

Latin: ancient language no longer in use except in scientific and scholarly circles

Malay: one of the languages of Malaysia

Miwok: one of the Native American languages

Navajo: one of the Native American languages

Osage: one of the Native American languages

Setswana: an African language

Sioux: one of the Native American languages

Swahili: a language spoken in Africa

Tupi: a native South American language

10 9 8 7 6 5 4 3 2 1

Published by Sterling Publishing Co., Inc.
387 Park Avenue South, New York, NY 10016
© 2003 by Evan and Lael Kimble
Distributed in Canada by Sterling Publishing
c/o Canadian Manda Group, One Atlantic Avenue, Suite 105
Toronto, Ontario, Canada M6K 3E7
Distributed in Great Britain by Chris Lloyd at Orca Book
Services, Stanley House, Fleets Lane, Poole BH15 3AJ, England
Distributed in Australia by Capricorn Link (Australia) Pty. Ltd.
P.O. Box 704, Windsor, NSW 2756, Australia

Printed in China
All rights reserved

Sterling ISBN 1-4027-0415-1

CONTENTS

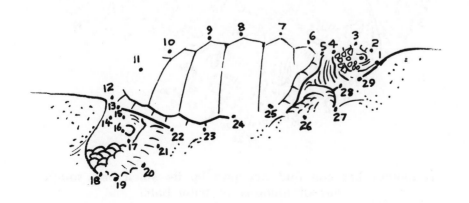

BAT

NAME: Babies are called pups.

TYPE OF ANIMAL: A bat is a mammal, which means it nurses on its mother, in this case for 6 weeks. Bats are the only mammals that can fly.

GROWING INSIDE: There are 900 different kinds of bats, so the amount of time the baby grows inside its mother can be anywhere between 2 and 9 months. One pup is born at a time, but sometimes there are twins or quadruplets.

SIZE AT BIRTH: Some are as small as your thumb and others no bigger than your hand.

WEIGHT AT BIRTH: As much as 1/4 of their mother's weight, which would be like a human mother having a 31-pound (14kg) baby!

GROWING UP: By about 3 months, the baby bat can fly and find food on its own. At 6 to 12 months a bat can have babies of its own.

WHERE IT LIVES: Bats are found almost everywhere on earth, except in extremely hot and extremely cold places.

SOUND IT MAKES: "Squeeeaaaaaaak, Squeeeaaaaaaak!"

YOU: Bats sleep upside down. What position do you like sleeping in?

**A mother bat can find her pup by its smell and sound
out of millions of baby bats!**

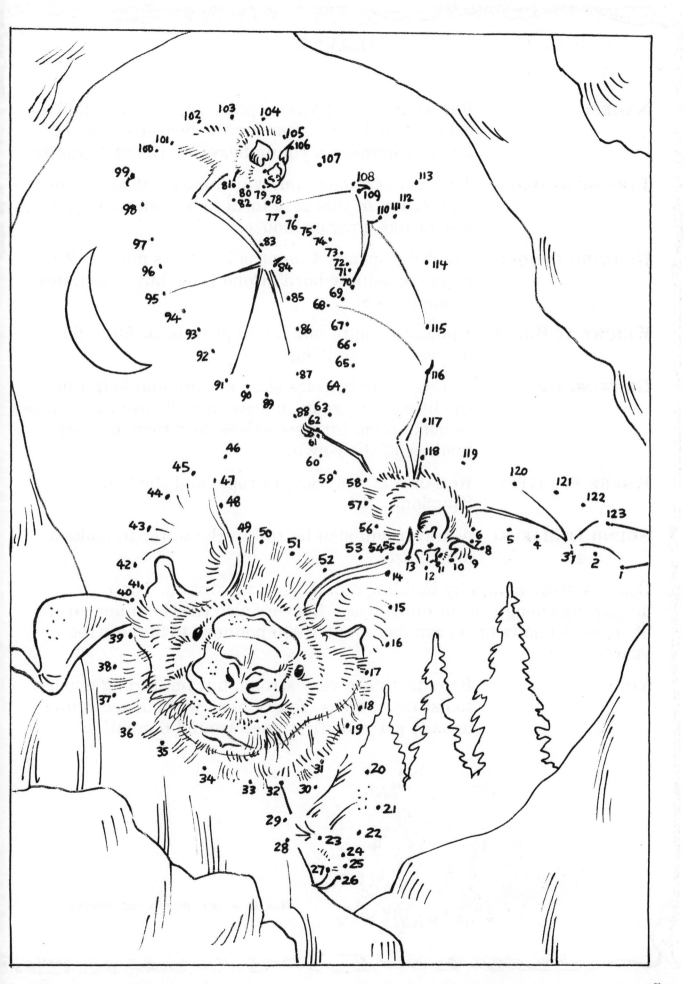

BEAVER

NAMES: Babies are called kits or pups. A group is called a colony. The Sioux name for the beaver is Chapa, and in Cherokee a young beaver is called Tayanita.

TYPE OF ANIMAL: A beaver is a mammal, which means it nurses on its mother, in this case for 2 to 3 months. It is a rodent like a rat or mouse.

GROWING INSIDE: The baby spends 4 months inside its mother. 2 to 4 pups are usually born at one time, but sometimes as many as 8!

WEIGHT AT BIRTH: 1 pound (.45kg), but it will grow to be 30 to 60 pounds (13.6 to 27kg).

GROWING UP: One-year-old beavers stick around and help raise the litter. Two-year-olds are kicked out of the lodge to make room for new babies, and they go start families of their own.

WHERE IT LIVES: Wetlands in America, Europe, and the United Kingdom.

SOUND IT MAKES: A beaver will slap its tail in the water to make a loud noise.

Beavers make homes by building a dam across a stream. Their teeth are strong enough to cut down trees. Beavers also eat the inner layers of trees. A family of six can eat about 1,000 pounds (454kg) of tree yearly.

YOU: Baby teeth are very strong, but not strong enough to cut down trees. You're born without teeth and usually get your first ones around 6 months.

This is a one month old beaver.

BLACK BEAR

NAMES: Babies are called cubs, mothers are called sows, and fathers are called boars. The Choctaw name for bear is Nita and the Miwok name is Uzumati.

TYPE OF ANIMAL: The Black Bear is a mammal, which means it nurses on its mother, in this case for about a year.

GROWING INSIDE: A black bear baby is inside its mother for 7 months but only grows for two of them. That's why it's so small. One to 5 babies are born at a time.

SIZE AT BIRTH: 5 inches (12.7cm), about as big as a stick of butter.

GROWING UP: The cubs stay with their mother for their first winter, and then they are on their own. At 3 years old they are ready to have cubs of their own.

WHERE IT LIVES: In the mountains and forests of North America and Asia.

SOUND IT MAKES: "GRRRRRRRRRRRRRRRR."

At the end of summer, bears will eat as much as they can. Then they enter a cave, a hollow log, or a hole in a tree and go into a deep sleep, during which they do not eat. This is called hibernation, and it can last from 4 to 7 months.

YOU: You were growing all the time inside your mother's belly. You never took a break like baby bears do.

When the bear grows up, it can weigh as much as 650 pounds (292.5kg).

9

BLUE WHALE

NAMES: Babies are called calves. Mothers are called cows, fathers are called bulls, and groups are called pods.

TYPE OF ANIMAL: A blue whale is a mammal, which means it nurses on its mother, in this case for 7 to 8 months. It is the largest mammal on earth.

GROWING INSIDE: The blue whale baby is inside its mother for 12 months. Only one is born at a time.

SIZE AT BIRTH: 20 to 25 feet (6 to 7.5m) long

WEIGHT AT BIRTH: 6,000 to 8,000 pounds (2,700 to 3,600kg)

GROWING UP: Within 30 minutes a baby blue whale can swim. At 6 to 10 years old, it can have babies of its own.

WHERE IT LIVES: In all the oceans of the world.

SOUND IT MAKES: Low moans, high squeals, whistles, and clicking noises that are sometimes put together in "songs" that can be heard underwater for miles. The whale repeats these songs over and over again, exactly the same as before. A blue whale is among the loudest animals in the world — louder than a jet plane.

During the first 7 months of its life, a blue whale gains 200 pounds (90kg) every 24 hours! It doesn't have any teeth at all. Instead, it has flat surfaces with ridges that filter tiny creatures from the water.

YOU: You didn't have all your baby teeth until you were around 3 years old.

The Blue Whale can blow water out of a blowhole on the top of its head. It can blow it as high as 20 feet (6m) in the air. That's a lot taller than you!

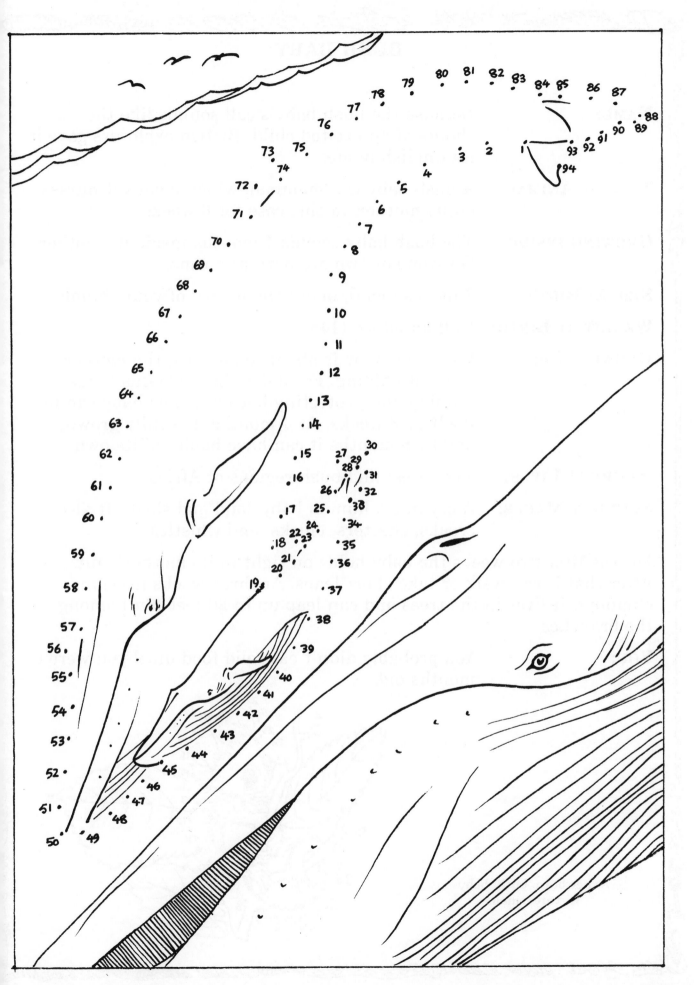

11

BUSH BABY

NAME: Because the bush baby's call sounds like the shouts of an excited child, British explorers gave it its English name.

TYPE OF ANIMAL: A bush baby is a mammal, which means it nurses on its mother, in this case for 6 weeks.

GROWING INSIDE: The bush baby spends 4 months inside its mother. Only one or two are born at a time.

SIZE AT BIRTH: 2 inches (5cm), about the length of your thumb.

WEIGHT AT BIRTH: Half an ounce (14g).

GROWING UP: When the baby is about to be born, the mother goes into hiding. For 3 days she remains hidden, nursing and protecting her baby. The baby can feed itself by 8 weeks. At 4 months it is fully grown, and by 8 months it can have babies of its own.

WHERE IT LIVES: The forest and bush regions of Africa.

SOUND IT MAKES: A cry like a human baby, loud and shrill. It also croaks, chatters, clucks, and whistles.

For the first two weeks the baby holds on tight to its mother's fur. After that it can walk or take short leaps. At three weeks it begins climbing. It lives in the trees and can leap up to 20 feet (6m) among the branches.

YOU: You probably didn't eat solid food until you were 6 months old.

A newborn bush baby is very small.

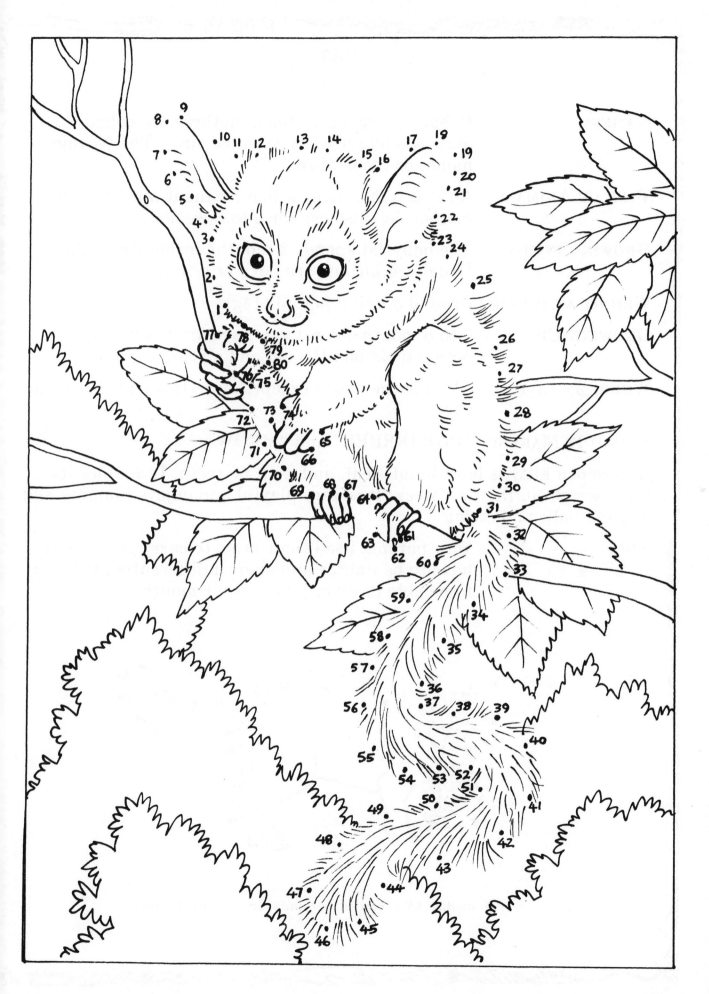

CAT

NAMES:	Babies are called kittens; mothers are called queens, and fathers are called sires. The Navajo name for cat is Mosi.
TYPE OF ANIMAL:	A cat is a mammal, which means it nurses on its mother, in this case for 6 to 8 weeks.
GROWING INSIDE:	The baby cat spends 2 months inside its mother. Usually, 4 kittens are born at a time.
WEIGHT AT BIRTH:	Around a half a pound (14g).
GROWING UP:	5 to 8 months. A cat can have kittens when between six months old and a year.
WHERE IT LIVES:	All over the world except Antarctica and the Arctic Circle.
SOUND IT MAKES:	"PURRRRRRR" and "MEOW."

A newborn kitty is born blind, deaf, and with no teeth. It doubles its birth weight in the first week. It is very playful and enjoys jumping and chasing balls and string.

YOU:	Your parents used their arms to carry you. You'd have to be lighter and shaped differently for them to be able to carry you in their mouth!

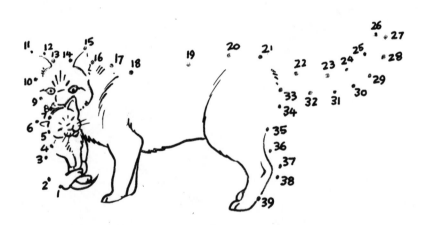

A mother kitty carries her little one in her mouth.

14

CHICKEN

NAMES: Babies are called chicks, mothers are called hens, and fathers are called roosters.

TYPE OF ANIMAL: A chick is a bird, which means it has feathers, a beak, and wings. It is born from an egg.

GROWING INSIDE: The chick grows in the egg for 22 days.

SIZE AT BIRTH: A little bigger than the egg you might find in your kitchen.

GROWING UP: A chick is born with very soft feathers, but starts to get new ones within a few days of hatching. A chick gets new feathers again about 3 months later and when it is ready to lay eggs.

WHERE IT LIVES: On farms all over the world.

SOUND IT MAKES: "Cheep, cheep, cheep." Grown chickens say, "Bok, bok, bok," and roosters say, "Cockadoodle doo!"

A baby bird is born with an egg tooth — a small notch on the front of its beak — which it uses to break out of the egg. Once it hatches, the chick loses the tooth. A chicken never does grow teeth. It uses its beak to grasp food and then it swallows it without chewing.

YOU: Human babies don't cheep. Usually they say, "WAHHHHHH!"

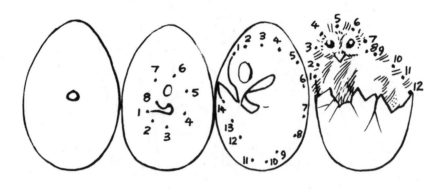

The chick grows, day by day, inside the shell of the egg.

CROCODILE

NAMES: A group of eggs is called a clutch, and babies are called hatchlings. Crocodiles have been around since before the dinosaurs, some 240 million years ago.

TYPE OF ANIMAL: A crocodile is a reptile, which means that it is scaly, cold-blooded, and almost always is born from an egg.

GROWING INSIDE: The hatchling grows inside the egg for 85 days.

SIZE AT BIRTH: 10 inches (25cm) long.

WEIGHT AT BIRTH: Less than 1 ounce (28g).

GROWING UP: The mother and father help the babies hack their way out of the egg. When crocodiles are 8 to 12 years old, they are ready to have their own babies. They can live to be 115 years old!

WHERE IT LIVES: Warm swamps, rivers, and marshes worldwide.

SOUND IT MAKES: High-pitched noises come from the eggs before they hatch. "Ptoooooh," "Hisssssssssssss," and "Cough!" Crocodiles make more noises than most reptiles. Some of them have 20 different messages that they say and understand.

YOU: You got a whole new set of teeth when you were about 6 years old. Crocodiles have different sets of teeth too, as many as 3,000 in a lifetime.

Here is a baby crocodile coming out of the egg.

DEER

NAMES: Babies are called fawns; mothers are called does; and fathers are called bucks. In Osage a fawn is called Niabi.

TYPE OF ANIMAL: A deer is a mammal, which means it nurses on its mother, in this case for 5 months.

GROWING INSIDE: The baby deer spends 200 days inside its mother. One to 4 fawns are born at a time.

WEIGHT AT BIRTH: 5 to 8 pounds (2.25 to 3.6kg), a little more than the weight of a sack of flour.

GROWING UP: A fawn stands within an hour or two of being born. If it's a buck the antlers start growing at 10 months old. A deer is able to have babies at about 2 years old but it does not reach its full growth until it is between 4 to 6 years of age.

WHERE IT LIVES: The open grasslands and woodland areas of North America, New Zealand, Europe, and the United Kingdom.

SOUND IT MAKES: Fawns bleat, and the mother calls them with a soft murmur.

YOU: You shed your old skin and grow new skin all the time. In fact, your body is completely new again every seven years.

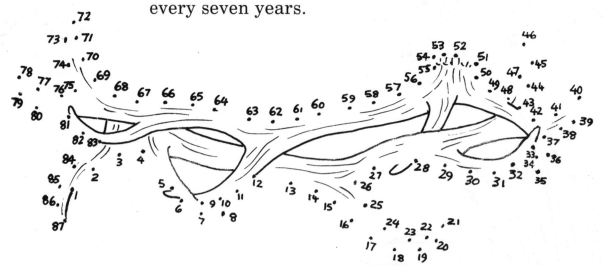

Bucks grow antlers, shed them, and then grow them again, kind of like a snake's skin. Here are some antlers that have been left behind.

DOG

NAMES: Dog babies are called puppies, mothers are called dams, and fathers are called sires. The Cheyenne have the word Honiahaka, meaning "little wolf."

TYPE OF ANIMAL: A dog is a mammal, which means it nurses on its mother, in this case for as long as people keep them together. In the wild, a dog will nurse for about 5 months.

GROWING INSIDE: The baby dog spends 63 days growing inside its mother. Three to 6 pups are born at a time.

SIZE AT BIRTH: Most puppies can fit in your hand, or if from a large dog, your two hands.

GROWING UP: A dog can have puppies of its own after a year.

WHERE IT LIVES: All over the world.

SOUND IT MAKES: Dogs bark, whine, and whimper.

A puppy loves toys just like human babies do. For the first 24 months, a puppy is teething, which means it's losing its teeth and getting new ones. This makes its gums ache and makes it want to get its teeth into something.

YOU: You probably liked to chew and teethe on things as a baby, just like puppies do.

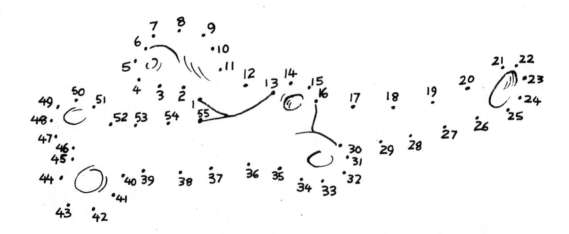

A puppy can work through teething with a toy like this.

DOLPHIN

NAMES:	Babies are called calves, groups are called pods.
TYPE OF ANIMAL:	A dolphin is a mammal, which means it nurses on its mother, in this case for 1 year.
GROWING INSIDE:	The baby dolphin spends a year growing inside its mother. Only one dolphin is born at a time.
WEIGHT AT BIRTH:	A newborn dolphin weighs 30 pounds (13.6kg), about as much as a two-year-old child. It will grow up to be around 200 pounds (90.7)! That's the weight of a grown man.
GROWING UP:	A calf nurses within 6 hours of being born, close to the surface of the water. It begins to eat fish at about 3 to 4 months, when its teeth come in. Females are ready to have babies when they are 5 to 7 years old, but males are not ready until they are 11.
WHERE IT LIVES:	Worldwide in oceans, except at the Poles.
SOUNDS IT MAKES:	Dolphins make whistling and clicking sounds. These sound like moans, trills, grunts, squeaks, and creaking doors. A calf can make sounds within a few days of birth.
YOU:	You could make sounds as soon as you were born, and most babies make a lot of them!

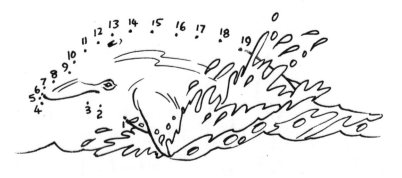

This is what the baby dolphin looks like.

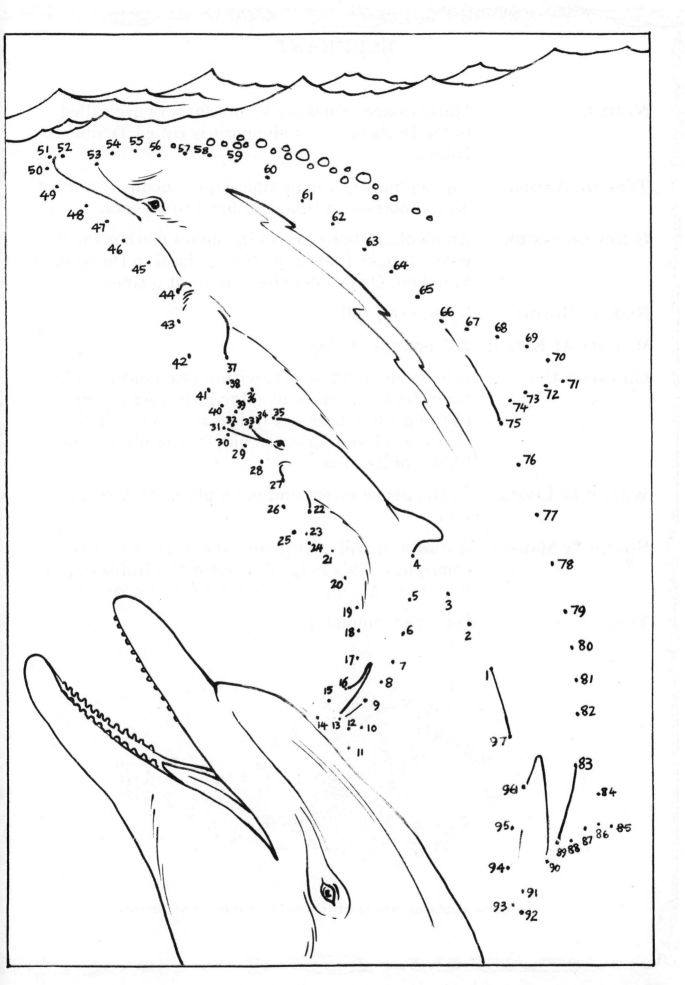

ELEPHANT

NAMES: Mothers are called cows, and fathers are called bulls. In Swahili, an elephant is called Tembo or Ndovu.

TYPE OF ANIMAL: An elephant is a mammal, which means it nurses on its mother, in this case for 2 to 5 years.

GROWING INSIDE: An elephant baby grows inside its mother for 2 years, longer than any other animal in the animal kingdom. Only one baby is born at a time.

SIZE AT BIRTH: 3 feet (1m) tall.

WEIGHT AT BIRTH: 265 pounds (120kg).

GROWING UP: A baby elephant stands within one hour of being born. Its tusks show at 30 months and it stops nursing when they get in the way. When it is between 11 and 15 years old, it is ready to make babies of its own.

WHERE IT LIVES: In the dense forest and open plains of Africa and Asia.

SOUND IT MAKES: A newborn will sneeze and snort when it first comes out. This helps it to clear the fluids out of its trunk. A baby will squeal when it needs help.

YOU: You are a mammal too.

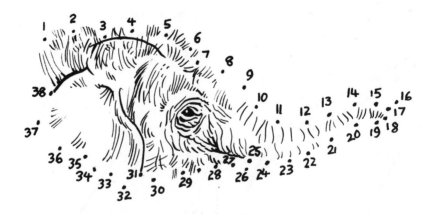

Baby elephants are much more hairy than their parents.

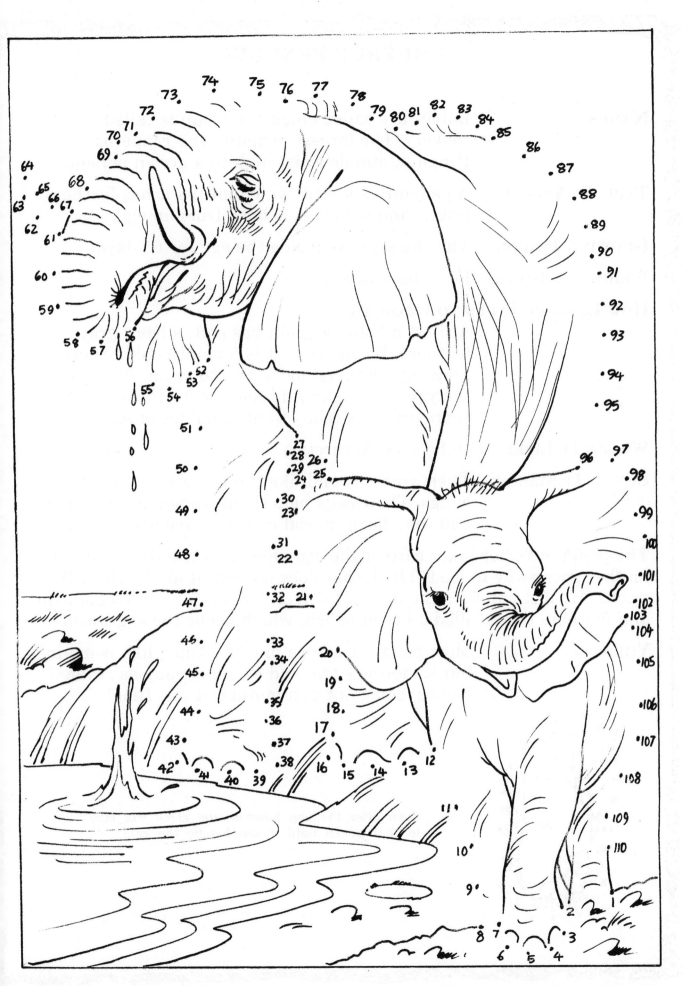

EMPEROR PENGUIN

NAMES: Babies are called chicks. A group is called a rookery. The largest penguin, the Emperor Penguin, stands waist high to a grown person.

TYPE OF ANIMAL: A penguin is a bird, which means it has feathers, beaks, and wings. It is born from an egg.

GROWING INSIDE: The chick grows inside the egg for 65 days.

WEIGHT AT BIRTH: Less than an ounce.

HOW LONG IT TAKES TO GROW UP:
At first a baby penguin has soft, silvery-gray feathers. By the time it is 5 months old, it has its grownup feathers and starts to swim. By 7 months, the young one can find food by itself. At 3 to 8 years old, it is ready to have babies of its own.

WHERE IT LIVES: In icy cold Antarctica.

SOUND IT MAKES: Their voices sound like the quick flapping of wings. Their calls help them recognize each other, and they have special calls to warn about danger.

The penguin father takes care of the egg almost all the time while the mother goes away to feed. The father does not eat at all for these 9 weeks. He just balances the egg on his feet. He has a thick roll of skin and feathers there called a brood pouch, which keeps the egg warm.

YOU: Most people are born one at a time, like penguins, but sometimes two and even as many as seven babies come out of a mother at one time!

Even after the egg hatches, the chick will stay in that pouch until it can handle the cold.

FROG

NAMES: Newly out of the egg, babies are called tadpoles, then froglets until they lose their tail. A group is called an army. The Cherokee name for spring frog is Tooantuh.

TYPE OF ANIMAL: A frog is an amphibian, which means that it lives both on land and in water.

GROWING INSIDE: The baby frog grows inside the egg for 3 to 6 days.

SIZE AT BIRTH: Smaller than your thumb.

GROWING UP: A tadpole will stay in the water for a few weeks to 2 years, depending on the type of frog, before it starts to change.

WHERE IT LIVES: Near lakes, ponds, and streams all over the world, except polar regions.

SOUND IT MAKES: A frog says, "Ribbit, ribbit!" and croaks. Some types of frog even have short, high-pitched whistles.

The frog lays eggs by a lily pad. Each tiny egg is wrapped in clear jelly. An egg hatches into a tadpole, and it breathes with gills like a fish, and swims using a tail. Then it starts to grow lungs, and its gills disappear. It grows legs, its tail is absorbed, and it becomes a frog. This change is called a "metamorphosis."

YOU: You were an egg once too, when you were still inside your mother.

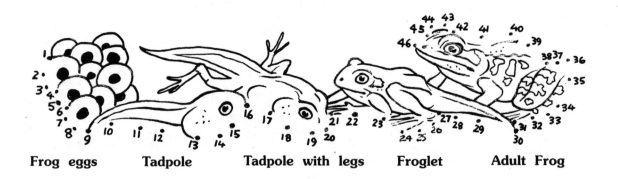

Frog eggs   Tadpole   Tadpole with legs   Froglet   Adult Frog

These are the stages a tadpole goes through before it becomes a frog.

GIRAFFE

NAMES: Babies are called calves, mothers are called cows, and fathers are called bulls. A group is called a herd. The giraffe's name in one African language means "food." It is named this because it eats a lot.

TYPE OF ANIMAL: A giraffe is a mammal, which means it nurses on its mother, in this case for 6 months.

GROWING INSIDE: The baby giraffe grows inside its mother for 15 months. Only one calf is born at a time.

SIZE AT BIRTH: 6 feet (1.8m) tall, about the size of a tall man. The tallest land animal in the world, it grows to be about 19 feet (5.7m) tall.

WEIGHT AT BIRTH: 130 pounds (58.5kg). But they grow to weigh as much as 2,800 pounds (1,260kg).

GROWING UP: A newborn giraffe will stand within minutes of being born. By the time the giraffe is 5, it is old enough to have its own babies.

WHERE IT LIVES: The savannahs and open bush country of Africa.

SOUND IT MAKES: "Snort," "moo," "bleat," and it grunts and bellows. Giraffes also talk by using their tail and by moving their neck and head in special ways.

YOU: A big giraffe can eat 75 pounds (33.75kg) of food in 24 hours! 75 pounds is probably more than you weigh!

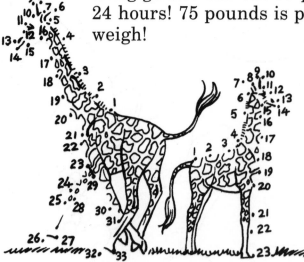

When giraffes swish their tail, it means they are excited. If they arch their tail, it means they're scared.

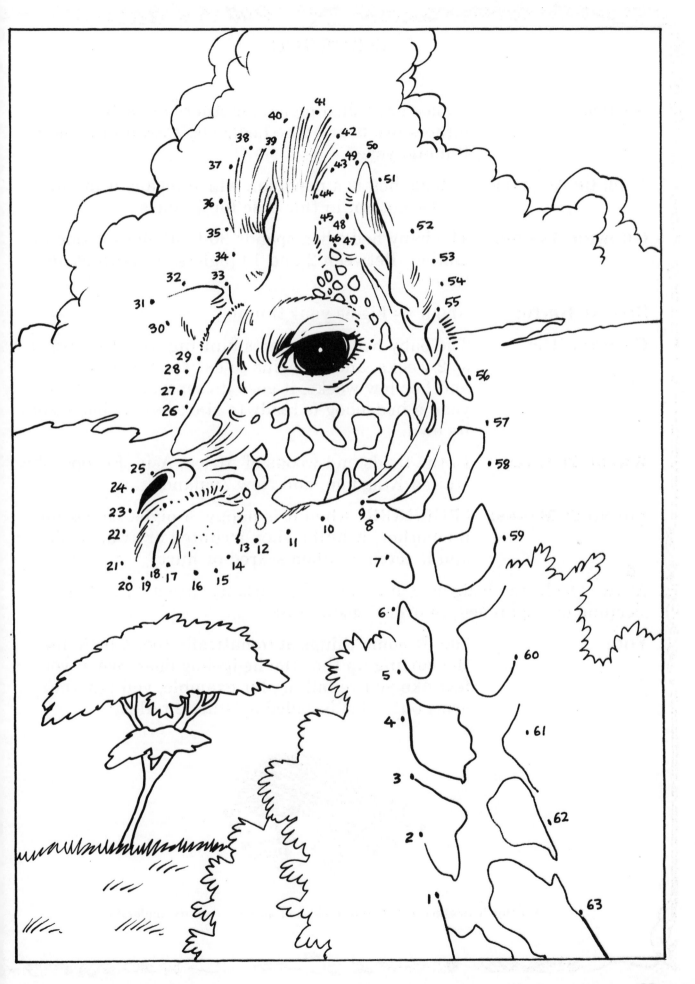

HEDGEHOG

NAMES: Babies are called piglets, mothers are sows, and fathers are boars. The hedgehog's Swahili name is Kalunguyeye.

TYPE OF ANIMAL: A hedgehog is a mammal, which means it nurses on its mother, in this case for 40 days.

GROWING INSIDE: The baby hedgehog spends 30 to 40 days inside its mother. Between 2 and 10 piglets are born at one time.

SIZE AT BIRTH: About as big as your thumb.

GROWING UP: The baby hedgehog starts hunting with its mother at 2 weeks, and it begins to eat solid food. In another few weeks, it goes its separate way. By one year, a hedgehog is ready to start having babies of its own.

WHERE IT LIVES: In the fields and woods of Africa, Asia, Europe, the United Kingdom, and New Zealand.

SOUND IT MAKES: "PURRRRR" when it is happy. A piglet chirps for its mother; it huffs when irritated or awakened, and it screams when scared or hurt.

At two weeks the hedgehog automatically curls up into a ball when it is sleeping or frightened, in order to stay safe.

YOU: You do some things automatically too, a little like the curling up that the hedgehog does. When you feel like you're falling, for example, you put your arms out. This is called a "startle reflex."

A baby hedgehog starts out pink and hairless on its underside.

HORSE

NAMES: Babies are foals; girls are fillies, boys are colts. Mothers are mares, and fathers are sires. When it is one year old, the horse is called a yearling. The Dakota name for horse is Tasunke.

TYPE OF ANIMAL: A horse is a mammal, which means it nurses on its mother, in this case for 4 to 6 months when living with people — but in the wild a baby horse will nurse for 2 years.

GROWING INSIDE: The baby horse grows inside its mother for 11 months. Only one foal is born at a time.

WEIGHT AT BIRTH: 100 to 175 pounds (45 to 78.75kg).

GROWING UP: A newborn foal can stand up within an hour of being born; it will walk, run, and trot within two hours. At 2 years old, it can have babies of its own.

WHERE IT LIVES: All over the world except in the Arctic and Antarctica.

SOUND IT MAKES: "Neeeeiiiiiighhhhhh," and whinnying sounds.

When a horse is born, its legs are almost their full adult length, giving them a cute "long-legged look." Most foals are born at night, away from possible danger.

YOU: You couldn't hold your head up until you were about 4 months old.

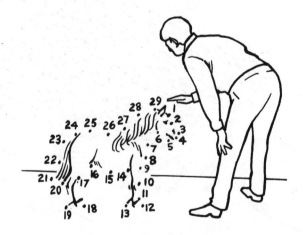

Horses even come in really small sizes. This is a miniature horse. It looks like a baby but is fully grown.

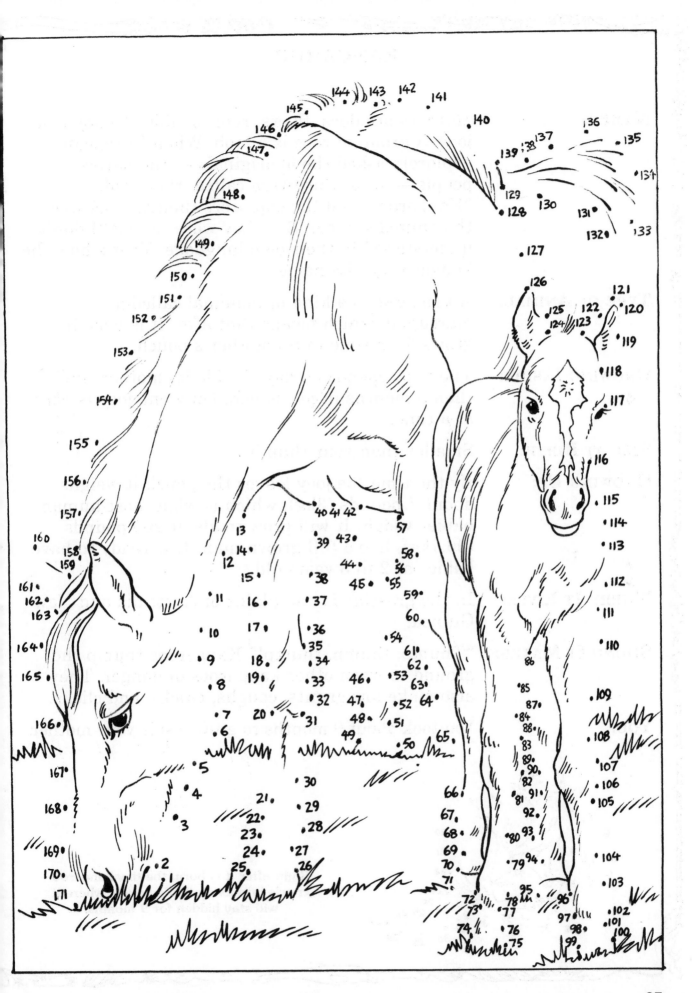

KANGAROO

NAMES: Mothers are does, flyers, roos, or jills. A baby is a joey. A group of roos is a mob. When European explorers asked the aboriginals — the native people — what they were called, they said, "Kangaroo," and the explorers thought this was the animal's name. But they were saying "I don't understand" in their own language. That's how the kangaroo got its name.

TYPE OF ANIMAL: A kangaroo is a kind of mammal called a marsupial, which means that after it is born it grows for a time in its mother's pouch.

GROWING INSIDE: The baby spends 36 days inside its mother, and then 9 months in her pouch. Only one joey is born at a time.

SIZE AT BIRTH: Smaller than your thumb.

GROWING UP: By the time the joey leaves the pouch it weighs about 7 pounds (3kg), which is what most human babies weigh. It will grow to about 200 pounds (90.7kg), like a full-grown man. It is ready to have babies at 2 to 3 years old.

WHERE IT LIVES: In the grasslands and plains of Australia and New Guinea.

SOUND IT MAKES: "Thump, thump, thump!" Kangaroos thump the ground to warn other kangaroos of danger. They also make low grunts, coughs, clucks, and clicks.

YOU: You took about 9 months to grow inside your mother.

Right after it is born, the tiny kangaroo crawls into its mother's pouch, where it will stay hidden for 9 months.

KOALA

NAMES:
Like the kangaroo, a koala baby is called a joey. The word "koala," thought to come from the language of the native Australian people, means "no drink."

TYPE OF ANIMAL:
A koala is a mammal, which means it nurses on its mother, in this case for a year. It is also a marsupial, which means that after it is born it grows for a long time in its mother's pouch.

GROWING INSIDE:
The baby koala spends 34 to 36 days inside its mother, then it lives for a year in its mother's pouch. Only one joey is born at a time.

SIZE AT BIRTH:
The size of a jelly bean.

WEIGHT AT BIRTH: Less than an ounce.

GROWING UP:
When the baby koala is born it looks like a pink jelly bean. It's totally hairless, blind, and has no ears. It stays with its mother for 3 or 4 years until it is full grown. Then the koala can make babies of its own.

WHERE IT LIVES:
The eucalyptus forests of Australia.

SOUND IT MAKES:
Males make a belching sound when attacked — almost like a lion's roar. Females make a sound like a human baby crying.

YOU:
You were probably carried in a kind of pouch too, a sling or a front pack, on your mother or father's belly when you were small. It's very cozy.

Here is a very young koala.

LEOPARD

NAMES: Babies are called cubs. In West Africa, a leopard is called Damissa.

TYPE OF ANIMAL: A leopard is a mammal, which means it nurses on its mother, in this case for 3 months.

GROWING INSIDE: The baby leopard spends 90 to 112 days inside its mother. Between 1 and 6 cubs are born at a time.

WEIGHT AT BIRTH: About one to 2 pounds (.45 to .9kg), but it will grow to be from 60 to 210 pounds (27 to 94.5kg).

GROWING UP: A baby leopard learns to walk at about 13 days. Between 18 and 24 months it is almost grown up and leaves its mother. At 2½ to 3 years, it can have cubs of its own.

WHERE IT LIVES: In the open plains, tropical forests, brush and shrub land, rocky hillsides, and woodlands of Africa, southern Asia, and the Middle East.

SOUND IT MAKES: "Huuuuummmmmmm": a 3-day-old leopard cub will hum while nursing. When it grows up it says, "RAAAAAR!"

YOU: You didn't learn to walk until you were about a year old.

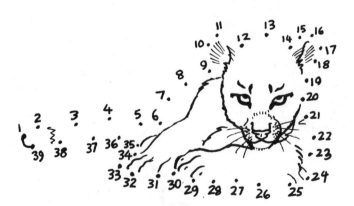

Here is a leopard at 6 weeks old. A newborn leopard has no spots, just light-colored fur.

LION

NAMES: Babies are cubs. A mother is a lioness. A group is called a pride. In Hindi, a lion is called a Sher, Untia Bagh, which means "camel tiger."

TYPE OF ANIMAL: A lion is a mammal, which means it nurses on its mother, in this case for 6 to 7 months.

GROWING INSIDE: The baby spends 3½ months growing inside its mother. Between 1 and 6 cubs are born at a time.

WEIGHT AT BIRTH: 2 to 4 pounds (.9 to 1.8kg)

GROWING UP: A cub's eyes are open at birth or open within the first two weeks. It is able to follow its mother at 3 months, and hunt with the group at 11 months. It can be on its own by 30 months, and can make babies when it is between 3 and 4 years old.

WHERE IT LIVES: In the open grass plains, savannahs, open woodlands, and scrub country of Africa and a small part of India.

SOUND IT MAKES: A "ROOOOAR" and at least 9 different sounds, including grunts.

A pride can be made up of about 40 lions, mostly mothers and babies, and one or 2 fathers — one very big close knit family.

YOU: Like a lion, you also could see right after you were born, but not very well — only general shapes in black and white.

The grownup lions look different from one another: fathers have a big mane and the mothers have short hair.

ORANGUTAN

NAMES: Babies are called infants. Orangutan means "man of the forest" in Indonesian and Malay. Orangutans are also called great apes and are our closest living wild animal relatives.

TYPE OF ANIMAL: An orangutan is a mammal, which means that it nurses on its mother, in this case for 3 years.

GROWING INSIDE: The baby spends 8 to 9 months inside its mother. Only one infant is born at a time.

WEIGHT AT BIRTH: 3 pounds (1.35kg).

GROWING UP: An infant screams loudly if separated from its mother. It clings to its mother's belly for its first year by gripping her fur; then it rides on her back until it's about 2½ years of age. It stays with its mother until she has another baby. This usually occurs when it is 6 to 8 years old. Then it leaves and begins a family of its own.

WHERE IT LIVES: In the trees of Sumatra and Borneo.

SOUND IT MAKES: Long calls, roars, and groans.

Orangutans sleep in their nests, usually a new one every evening. They also build nests in the daytime to rest and play in. A mother with young children might build 2 or 3 nests a day.

YOU: As a baby you had a special play area too that your parents made for you. Do you still have a special place like that?

A nest is woven in the branch of a tree and is usually very well made, like a big basket.

OSTRICH

NAMES: Babies are called chicks, mothers are called hens, and fathers are called roosters. The Setswana name for ostrich is Mmantshe.

TYPE OF ANIMAL: An ostrich is a bird, which means it has feathers, a beak, and wings, and is born from an egg. It is a type of bird that doesn't fly.

GROWING INSIDE: The ostrich baby spends 42 days growing in the egg.

WEIGHT AT BIRTH: About 3 pounds (1.35kg).

GROWING UP: An ostrich can have babies of its own when it is between 3 and 4 years old.

WHERE IT LIVES: The open savannah and wide plains of Africa.

SOUND IT MAKES: A loud hiss or booming roar.

An ostrich buries its head in the sand to see if its eggs are still there and safe. Both the mother and father birds sit on the egg, which is so strong that a large person could stand on it, and it wouldn't break. That's so it can hold up against the weight of the ostrich, which is around 285 pounds (128kg) — twice the size of an adult.

YOU: You come from an egg that's much much smaller than a canteloupe. It's so small that even if you could see inside your mother's body, it would be too small for your eyes to see.

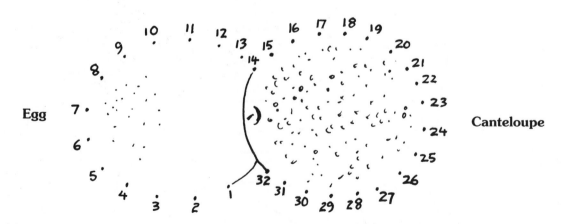

The ostrich egg is the biggest of all the birds. It can weigh up to 4½ pounds (2kg) and is as big as a cantaloupe.

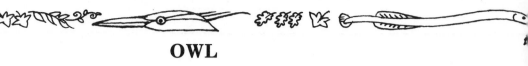

OWL

NAMES: Babies are called owlets, and a nest of eggs or brood of them is called a clutch. Their Navajo name is Nascha.

TYPE OF ANIMAL: An owl is a bird, which means it has feathers, beaks, and wings, and is born from an egg.

GROWING INSIDE: The baby owl spends 3 months growing in the egg.

WEIGHT AT BIRTH: At birth, owlets weigh a little more than 1 pound (.45kg), which is about as much as four sticks of butter.

GROWING UP: Owlets can't see for about 15 days. At 3 weeks of age, the nestlings hop from the nest and climb the nearby trees and shrubs. At 8 weeks, the owlets can make short flights. By the time they are 2 years old, they are ready to make babies.

WHERE IT LIVES: North, Central, and South America, Europe, the United Kingdom, North Africa, and Central Asia.

SOUND IT MAKES: "Hoo-Hoo-Hoo."

Owls are nocturnal, which means that they sleep during the day and stay awake at night. Their eyes are able to take in lots of light, so no matter how dark it is, they can still see.

YOU: Your eyes change when the lights go out. The black part of your eyeball gets bigger to let in more light, so that you can see more.

Owls can't move their eyes, but they can move their necks so much that they can look all the way behind them.

51

PANDA

NAMES: Babies are called cubs. "Xiongmao," the Chinese name for the giant panda, means "giant cat bear."

TYPE OF ANIMAL: A panda is a mammal, which means it nurses on its mother, in this case for 8 or 9 months.

GROWING INSIDE: The baby panda spends 3 to 5½ months growing inside its mother. One or two cubs are born at a time.

SIZE AT BIRTH: 28 inches (70cm)

WEIGHT AT BIRTH: 4 ounces (112g), smaller than a mouse.

GROWING UP: By the 5th month, the young panda is walking, running, and playing, and it starts eating bamboo, the main food of pandas. It stays with its mother for about 18 months and is able to have its own babies when it is around 6 years old.

WHERE IT LIVES: The mountain forests of China.

SOUND IT MAKES: The newborn has a very loud voice for its size. It sounds like a bleating sheep. Pandas also honk, squeal, growl, moan, and bark.

A baby panda is very small; the mother is at least 800 times bigger. If your mother was that much bigger than you when you were born she'd weigh 6,400 pounds (2903kg)! That's as big as a small elephant!

YOU: Like the baby panda, you weren't born with much hair either — no hair on your body, and only a bit on your head.

newborn

3 weeks old

The newborn panda is pink with white hair. Then it gets more hair, but it is three weeks old before it looks like its mother.

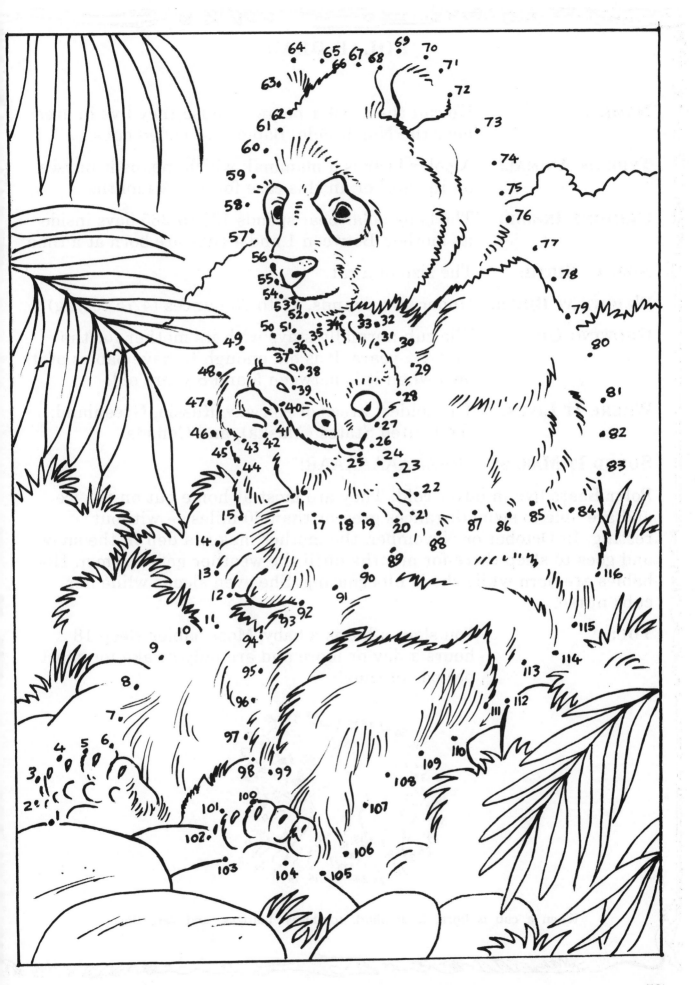

POLAR BEAR

NAMES: We call them polar bears because they live in areas near the North Pole. Babies are called cubs.

TYPE OF ANIMAL: A polar bear is a mammal, which means it nurses on its mother, in this case for 7 to 9 months.

GROWING INSIDE: The baby polar bear spends 195 to 265 days inside its mother. Between 1 and 4 cubs are born at a time.

SIZE AT BIRTH: The size of a rat.

WEIGHT AT BIRTH: Under two pounds, 17 to 25 ounces (4.75 to 7kg).

GROWING UP: The cub normally stays with its mother for the first 2½ years. It is old enough to have babies of its own when it is between 5 and 8 years old.

WHERE IT LIVES: The coldest areas of Norway, Russia, Greenland, the United States (Alaska), and Canada.

SOUND IT MAKES: "RAAAAAAAAAAR!"

Polar Bears live in bitter cold. They are most at home out on the ice and are able to swim distances greater than 60 miles — without resting. In October or November, the mother makes a den in the snow and goes to sleep there for months until the weather gets warmer. Her babies are born while she is hibernating. She even sleeps while her cubs nurse.

YOU: You slept a lot as a baby. Most babies sleep 18 hours a day or more and are only awake for short periods of time!

When a cub is born, it is blind, toothless, hairless, and very tiny.

RABBIT

NAMES: Babies are called bunnies, kits, or pups; mothers are does, fathers are bucks, and a group is called a herd. A Native American name for the rabbit is Lulu.

TYPE OF ANIMAL: A rabbit is a mammal, which means it nurses on its mother, in this case for 6 weeks.

GROWING INSIDE: The baby rabbit spends 31 days inside its mother. Between 2 and 8 bunnies are born at a time.

SIZE AT BIRTH: 2½ inches (6cm), easily fitting into the palm of your hand.

WEIGHT AT BIRTH: 2½ ounces (70g).

GROWING UP: A bunny does not spend much time with its mother. It gets nursed only once a day, and this may be the only time that mother and child spend together. It can eat solid food by 5 weeks. At 3 to 8 months, a bunny can make more bunnies.

WHERE IT LIVES: The fields and forests of the U.S., Canada, Central and South America, Europe, the United Kingdom, Australia, New Zealand, and Northern Africa.

SOUNDS IT MAKES: Cries, squeals, grunts, and it also thumps the ground with its feet to make a warning noise.

A rabbit nest is built out of the hair that a mother pulls off her belly!

YOU: Your nest — the place where you sleep — is probably a bed. But when you were younger it may have been a crib, a basinet, or maybe a cradle.

This is a bunny at 6 weeks. A kit's eyes open at about 2 weeks of age.

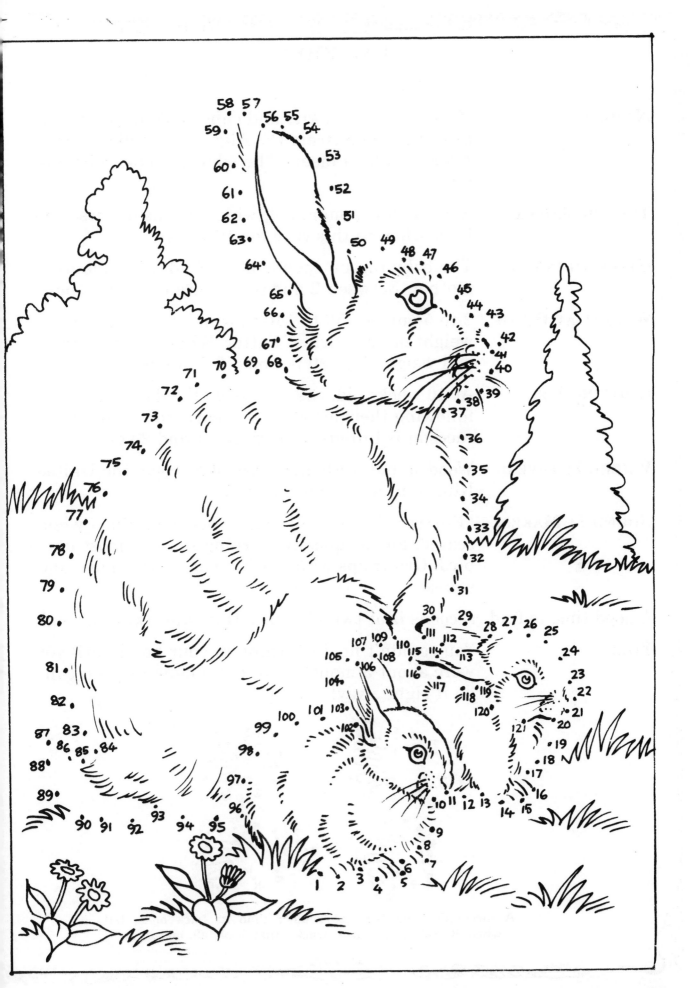

RACCOON

NAMES: Babies are called kits and cubs. The name raccoon probably comes from the Algonquin Indian word Arukun, which means "he who scratches with his hands."

TYPE OF ANIMAL: A raccoon is a mammal, which means it nurses on its mother, in this case for 16 weeks.

GROWING INSIDE: The baby racoon spends 63 to 65 days inside its mother. Between 2 and 5 cubs are born at a time.

WEIGHT AT BIRTH: 2 to 5 ounces (56 to 140g), which is about the weight of one stick of butter. When it grows up it will weigh 15 to 20 pounds (6.75 to 9kg).

GROWING UP: At 10 weeks old, the kits leave the den, start following their mother, and learn how to hunt. A raccoon is full-grown between 1 and 2 years.

WHERE IT LIVES: Wooded and wetlands areas of Europe, the United Kingdom, Asia, and America.

SOUND IT MAKES: "Purrrrrr," when nursing; "Waaaaahhhhh," when scared, and a squeaky chirping sound almost like a bird. Grownups whine, whimper, chirp, snarl, and squeal.

A good time to find raccoons is at twilight since they stay awake at night.

YOU: You couldn't hold anything in your hand until you were about 3 months old, but a baby raccoon can do it right away!

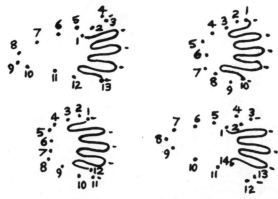

A raccoon's front feet are smaller than its back ones, but when it walks, it leaves tracks that look all mixed up.

59

RATTLESNAKE

NAMES: Babies are called neonates. The Algonquin name for snake is Askook.

TYPE OF ANIMAL: A rattlesnake is a reptile, which means that it is scaly, cold-blooded, and almost always is born from an egg.

GROWING INSIDE: The baby snake spends 110 days in the egg.

SIZE AT BIRTH: 10 inches (25cm), but they will grow to be 3 to 5 feet (.9 to 1.5m) long.

GROWING UP: A young rattler doesn't need its mother even right after it is born. At 2 to 3 years, a rattlesnake will make babies of its own.

WHERE IT LIVES: The prairie and rocky regions of North and South America.

SOUND IT MAKES: "HISSSSSSSSSSSS and "BUZZZZZZZZZZZ" and "Rattle, rattle, rattle."

After 7 to 10 days a newborn rattlesnake sheds its baby skin and adds its first rattle.

YOU: Even though they are so wiggly, the snake has a skeleton, just like you. A skeleton is a bunch of bones inside your body that help you move. You had a skeleton even before you were born.

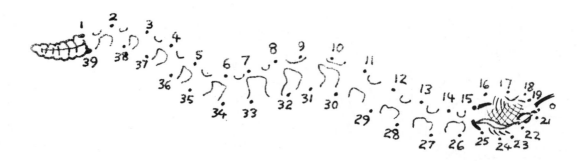

Grownup rattlers may have as many as 10 rattles, because they add a new one every year when they shed their skin.

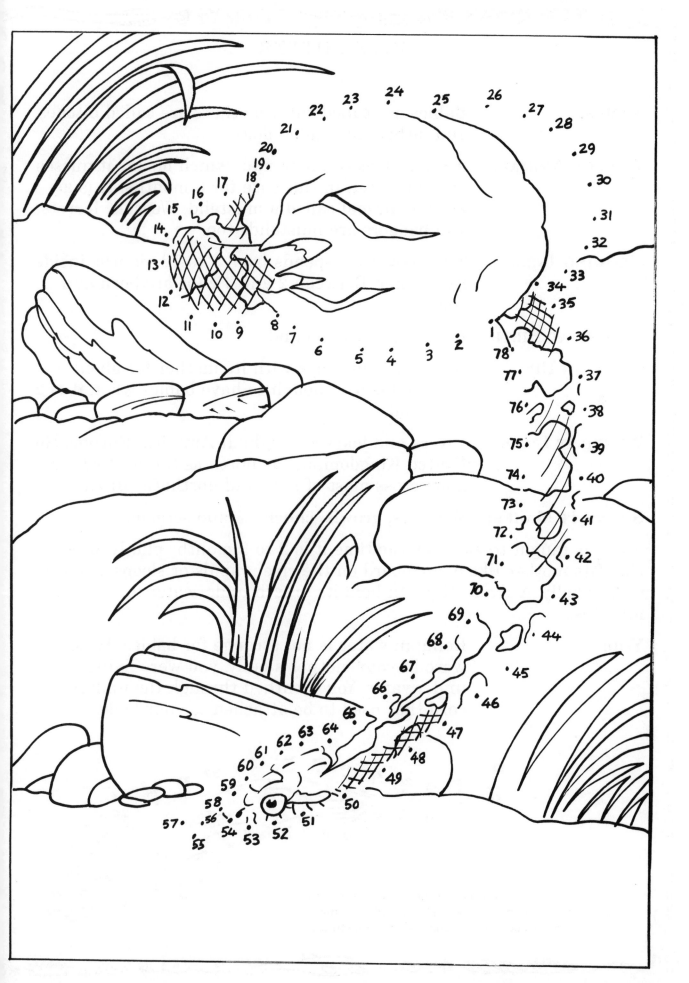

RIVER OTTER

NAMES: Babies are called cubs, mothers are called bitches, and fathers are called dogs.

TYPE OF ANIMAL: A river otter is a mammal, which means it nurses on its mother, in this case for 6 months. It is a kind of animal called a mustelid. Weasels, ferrets, and badgers are mustelids too.

GROWING INSIDE: The baby otter spends from 9 to 12 months inside its mother. Between 2 and 4 cubs are born at a time.

WEIGHT AT BIRTH: Less than half a pound.

GROWING UP: An otter baby stays with its mother for about a year and is old enough to have babies when it is 2 years old.

WHERE IT LIVES: Rivers and lakes throughout America, Europe, the United Kingdom, as far north as the Arctic Circle, and across most of Asia and northern Africa.

SOUND IT MAKES: Whistles, growls, chuckles, and screams.

A cub is taught to swim by the time it is 2 to 3 months old. It often rides its mother like a surfboard on the river rapids or sleeps soundly on her belly. A river otter can hold its breath underwater for up to 8 minutes.

YOU: Being in water is not strange for babies. When you were in your mother's belly, you were living underwater. You breathed through the umbilical cord that used to be attached to your belly.

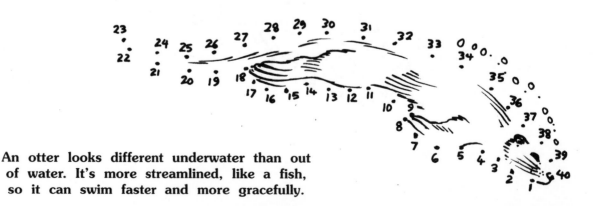

An otter looks different underwater than out of water. It's more streamlined, like a fish, so it can swim faster and more gracefully.

SALMON

NAMES:	Baby salmon are called alevins, then when they become small fish they're called fry or parr. Salmon are called Haloke in the Navajo language.
TYPE OF ANIMAL:	Fish
GROWING INSIDE:	The baby salmon spends 3 months inside the egg.
SIZE AT BIRTH:	2 inches (5cm), which is about the size of your thumb.
GROWING UP:	After it leaves the egg, the salmon is a tiny alevin, a little fish with a yoke sac attached to it. It drinks from this for about two weeks and then becomes a fry. As it gets ready for the ocean it changes color and gets silvery. These changes take from 1 to 7 years.
WHERE IT LIVES:	In all the cold waters of the northern hemisphere.

Eggs are laid in the bottom of the river and after they hatch, the salmon prepare for the ocean, getting ready to handle salt water. They spend up to six years at sea. Once they have grown up, they will somehow find their way back to the exact same stream from which they were hatched. They can travel up to 1,000 miles!

YOU:	First, you start out as an infant, then you become a toddler (when you start walking); after that you are a child or a kid; then you become a teenager, and then a grownup person.

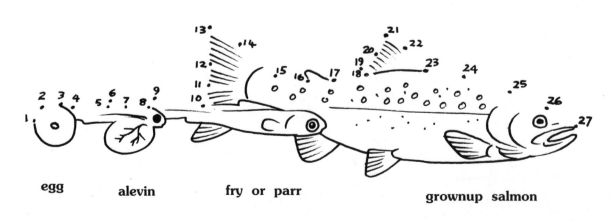

egg   alevin   fry or parr   grownup salmon

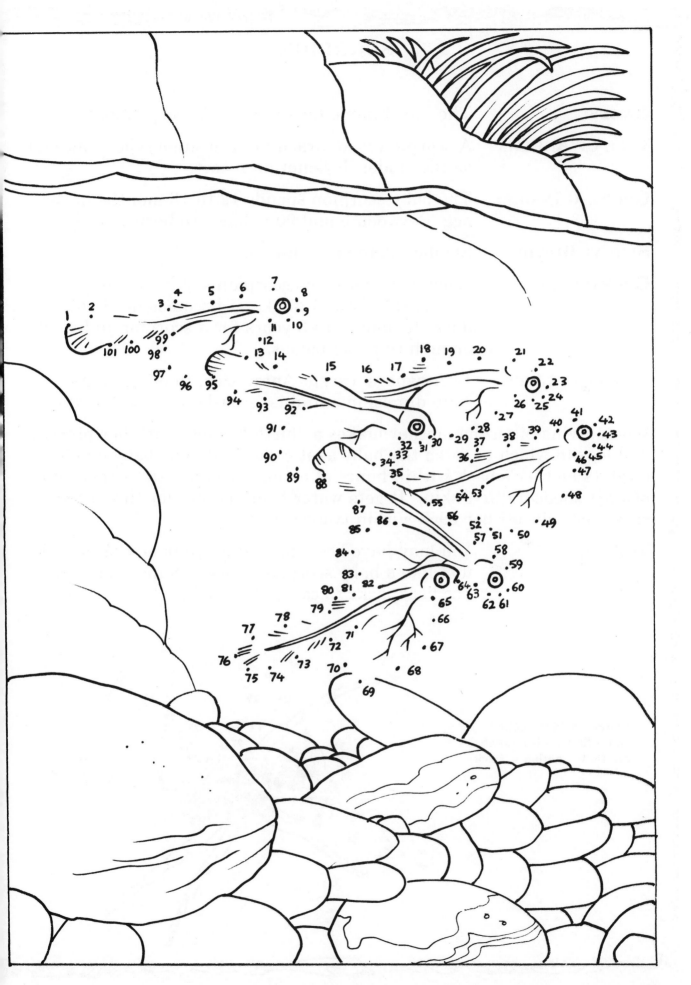

SCORPION

NAMES:	The Latin name for scorpion is scorpionidae.
TYPE OF ANIMAL:	A scorpion is an arachnid, the same type of animal as the spider. It is not an insect.
GROWING INSIDE:	The baby scorpion spends 12 to 18 months in the egg. Between 6 and 90 babies are born at a time.
SIZE AT BIRTH:	Smaller than your thumb.
GROWING UP:	When it is born, the scorpion's skin is white and soft. After about 4 weeks, it becomes hard and dark. It takes 1 to 3 years for a scorpion to be old enough to make babies.
WHERE IT LIVES:	Everywhere, except Antarctica, in desert flats, sand dunes, mountains, grasslands, and forests.

When giving birth the mother makes a "birth basket" with her pincers and legs in which to catch the baby as it comes out. The baby climbs onto its mother's back within hours of being born, and stays there until after it sheds its first skin. It gets water from its mother through her skin, and falls off her back within two weeks.

YOU:	You may have been carried on your mother's back just like a baby scorpion. Lots of human mothers use backpacks to carry their babies.

Spider babies, called spiderlings, also climb on their mother's back.

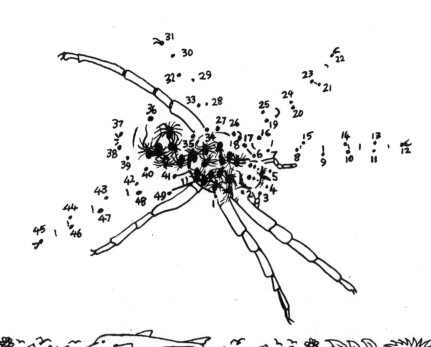

SEA HORSE

NAMES: Babies are called fry or ponies.

TYPE OF ANIMAL: A sea horse is a fish, which means it lives in the water and has bones that keep its shape.

GROWING INSIDE: The baby sea horse spends 10 to 60 days in its father's pouch, depending on the species. Usually about 400 ponies — but up to 2,000 — can be born at one time.

WEIGHT AT BIRTH: Less than an ounce.

GROWING UP: At 6 months, it is born fully formed and is on its own.

WHERE IT LIVES: All over the world in warm waters.

SOUND IT MAKES: A crackling sound when it's eating.

The mother lays the eggs and puts them into the father's pouch near his stomach where he fertilizes them. Each baby has its own little pouch where it gets what it needs from the father's bloodstream.

YOU: Many human fathers are the ones who take care of babies too.

There are 50 different species of sea horse, different shapes and sizes. The smallest one is less than 1 inch (2.5cm) tall, whereas the largest is over 1 foot (30cm) tall.

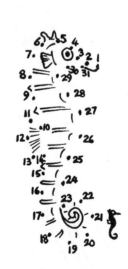

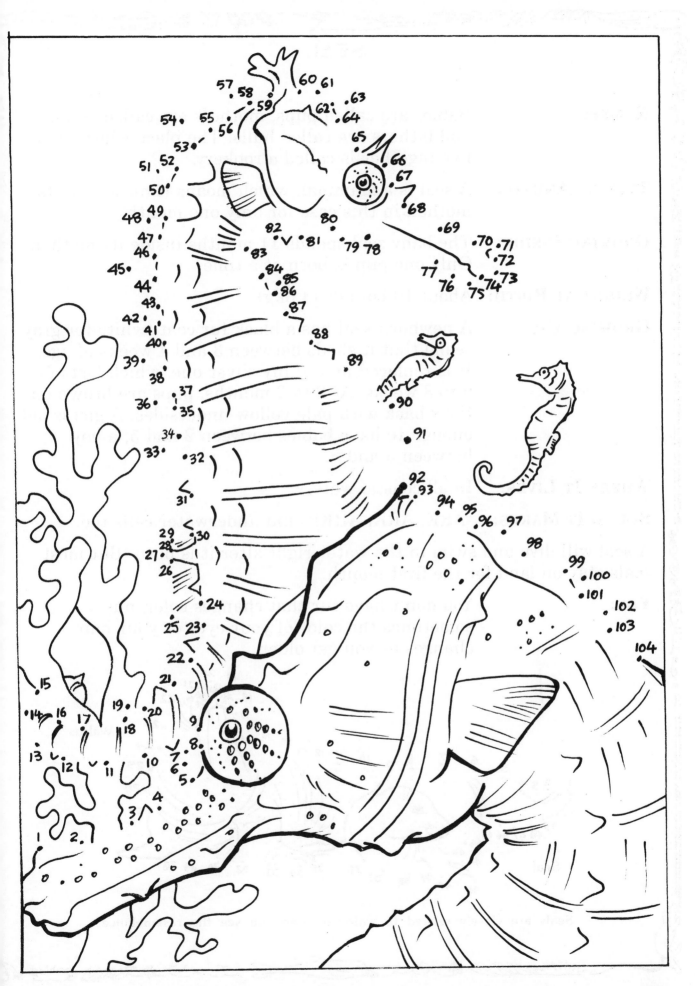

SEAL

NAMES: Babies are called pups, mothers are called cows, and fathers are called bulls. The place where they live together is called a rookery.

TYPE OF ANIMAL: A seal is a mammal, which means it nurses on its mother, in this case for only one month.

GROWING INSIDE: The baby seal spends 11 months inside its mother. Only one pup is born at a time.

WEIGHT AT BIRTH: About 10 pounds (4.5kg)

GROWING UP: A newborn seal has a black fur coat (white for gray seals) that it sheds between 3 and 4 weeks of age. It is replaced by a shiny silver one, which lasts for 6 to 8 weeks. At 2 to 3 months, pups are brown on their back with pale yellow undersides. A girl is old enough to have babies between 2 and 5, a boy between 3 and 6.

WHERE IT LIVES: In all coastal waters.

SOUND IT MAKES: "ARK, ARK, ARK!" and underwater calls too.

A seal will dive and swim in the water right after it is born. But most seals stay on land for the first month.

YOU: You don't have fur that changes color, but sometimes the color of your eyes or your hair changes as you get older.

Seals are closely related to walruses. Can you see the resemblance?

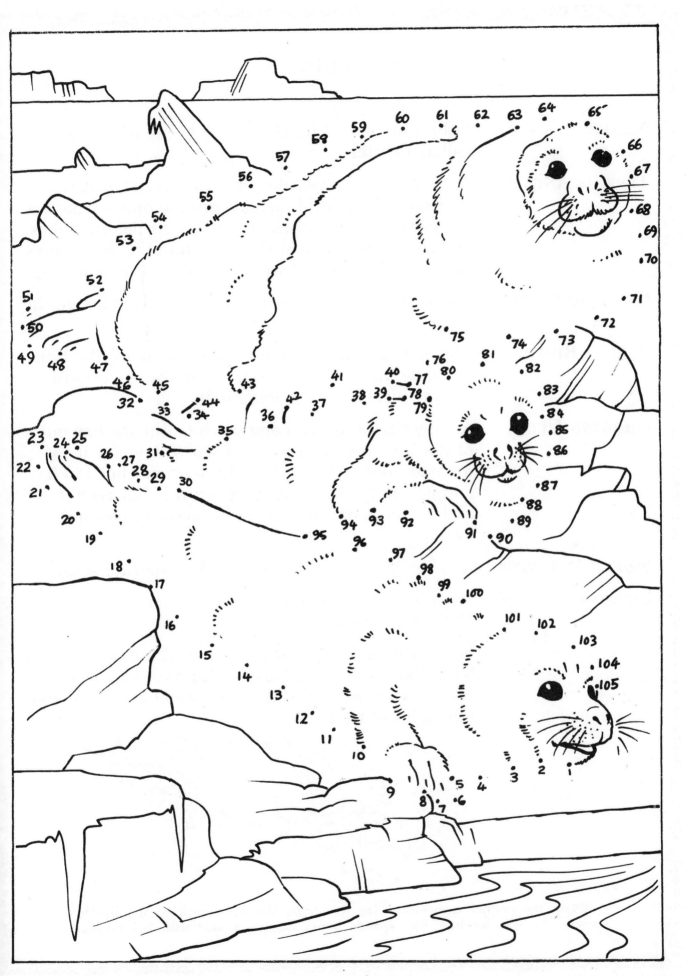

SEA TURTLE

NAMES: Babies are called hatchlings. A group of eggs is called a clutch.

TYPE OF ANIMAL: A sea turtle is a reptile, which means that it is cold-blooded. A cold-blooded animal doesn't have a temperature that works from the inside, but takes on the temperature of the air around it. So it stays in warm areas of the world. It is born from an egg.

GROWING INSIDE: The baby sea turtle spends 50 to 78 days inside the egg.

SIZE AT BIRTH: The eggs are different sizes depending on the type of turtle. Some are the size of an orange; others are the size of a Ping-Pong ball.

GROWING UP: A baby turtle uses an egg tooth to cut its way out of the egg, and then it takes 3 to 7 days for it to dig itself out of the sand, where its mother hid it, and get up to the surface. When it is between 3 and 10 years old, it is ready to make babies of its own.

WHERE IT LIVES: All over the world in warm and temperate seas.

SOUND IT MAKES: "Squeeaaaak" inside the egg and "Hisssssssssssssssssss."

YOU: You never had to dig yourself out of a hole as a baby, like turtles do, but you did have to learn to roll over, crawl, and walk. This was hard work and took a lot of time.

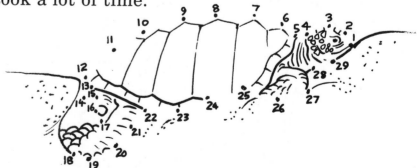

When the mother is ready to lay her eggs, she goes back to the beach where she was hatched. She spends hours digging a nest with her flippers.

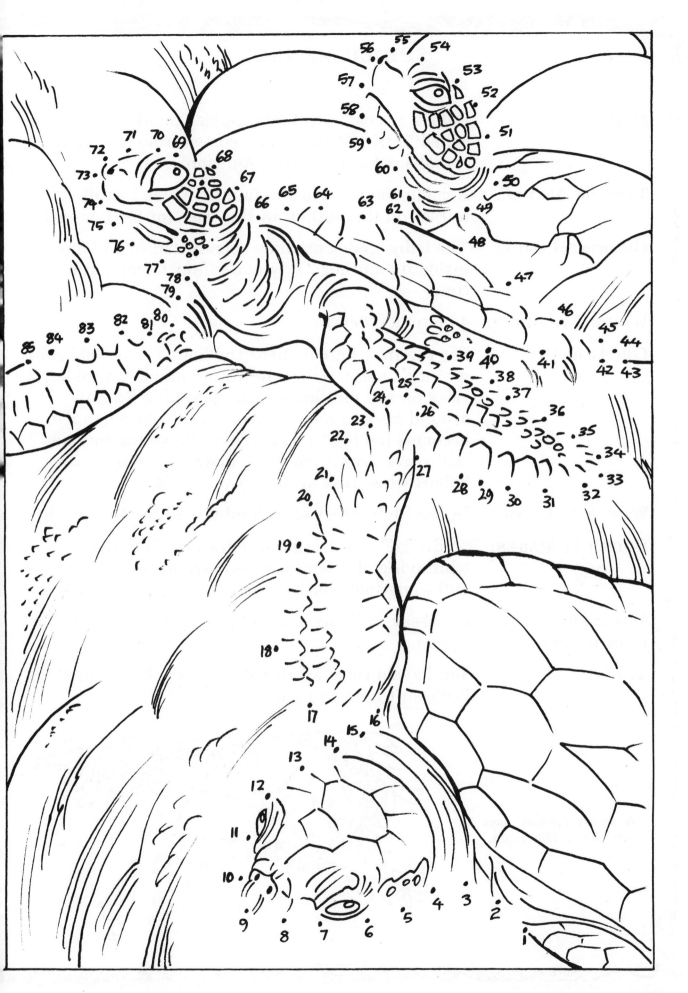

SPIDER MONKEY

NAMES: Babies are called infants. Spider monkeys are also called Muriqui: this name comes from the Tupi Indians, who live in the Amazon.

TYPE OF ANIMAL: A spider monkey is a mammal, which means it nurses on its mother, in this case for 6–10 months.

GROWING INSIDE: The baby spider monkey spends 226 to 232 days inside its mother. Only one infant is born at a time.

WEIGHT AT BIRTH: 4 pounds (10cm).

GROWING UP: For the first four months the baby is carried on its mother's belly. When the young monkey is older, it rides on the mother's back, wrapping its tail around hers to make it feel safe. Even when it becomes too big to be carried, the young monkey still stays very close to its mother. It has its own babies when it is around 5 years old.

WHERE IT LIVES: In the high forest of Columbia and South America.

SOUND IT MAKES: "NEIGH!": loud calls, which sound like the whinnying of a horse. When afraid, these monkeys will sometimes bark or make a coughing noise.

The spider monkey will break off heavy branches and drop them from trees to scare off intruders.

YOU: You have a tiny tail called a coccyx. Unfortunately, it doesn't help you climb.

A spider monkey uses its tail like a fifth hand.

TAPIR

NAMES: The name tapir comes from a native tribe in the Amazon, the Tupi. They called this animal Tapyra.

TYPE OF ANIMAL: A tapir is a mammal, which means it nurses on its mother, in this case for 6 to 8 months.

GROWING INSIDE: The baby tapir spends 13 months inside its mother. Only one baby is born at a time.

WEIGHT AT BIRTH: 15 to 25 pounds (6.75 to 11.25kg), and it will grow to be 550 to 660 pounds (225 to 297kg).

GROWING UP: Solid food becomes part of the young tapir's diet after only a few weeks. When it stops nursing it leaves its mother and goes off on its own. At 2 to 4 years old it's ready to make babies of its own.

WHERE IT LIVES: The rainforests in South and Central America, Malaysia, Burma, and Thailand.

SOUND IT MAKES: Squealing, clicking, and a shrill whistling call.

A tapir baby looks like a brown watermelon with whitish stripes and spots. It loses this baby coat within 4 to 7 months, and then it looks just like its parents who have no stripes, and are pinkish-brown.

YOU: You look like your parents and grandparents because you are related to them. They are made out of the same stuff as you. We call it having the same genes.

Two of these animals are relatives of the tapir. Can you guess which ones?

The horse and the rhinoceros.

ZEBRA

NAMES: Babies are called foals, mothers are called mares, and fathers are called stallions. Its Swahili name is Punda Milia.

TYPE OF ANIMAL: A zebra is a mammal, which means it nurses on its mother, in this case for a little over a year.

GROWING INSIDE: The baby zebra spends 12 to 13 months inside its mother. Only one foal is born at a time.

WEIGHT AT BIRTH: When it is born a baby zebra weighs 55 to 70 pounds (24.75 to 31.5kg), about as much as a 7 or 8 year-old child. By the time it grows up, it will weigh between 600 and 800 pounds (270 and 360kg).

GROWING UP: Right after birth, the foal can stand on its own. It can run within a day, and graze within a week. It is fully grown and can have babies of its own when it is between 2 and 4 years old.

WHERE IT LIVES: In Africa, on mountain slopes and grassy plains.

SOUND IT MAKES: A hoarse "ha-kwa, ha-kwa, ha kwa"— like a cross between a donkey's bray and a horse's whinny.

The foal learns how to tell who is its mother by her looks, her voice, and her smell. It has brown stripes. No two sets of stripes on a zebra are the same!

YOU: As a baby you could tell who your mother was by her smell.

When grooming itself, the zebra is particularly fond of rolling in mud. When the mud dries and is shaken off, loose hair and dry skin are pulled away.

INDEX